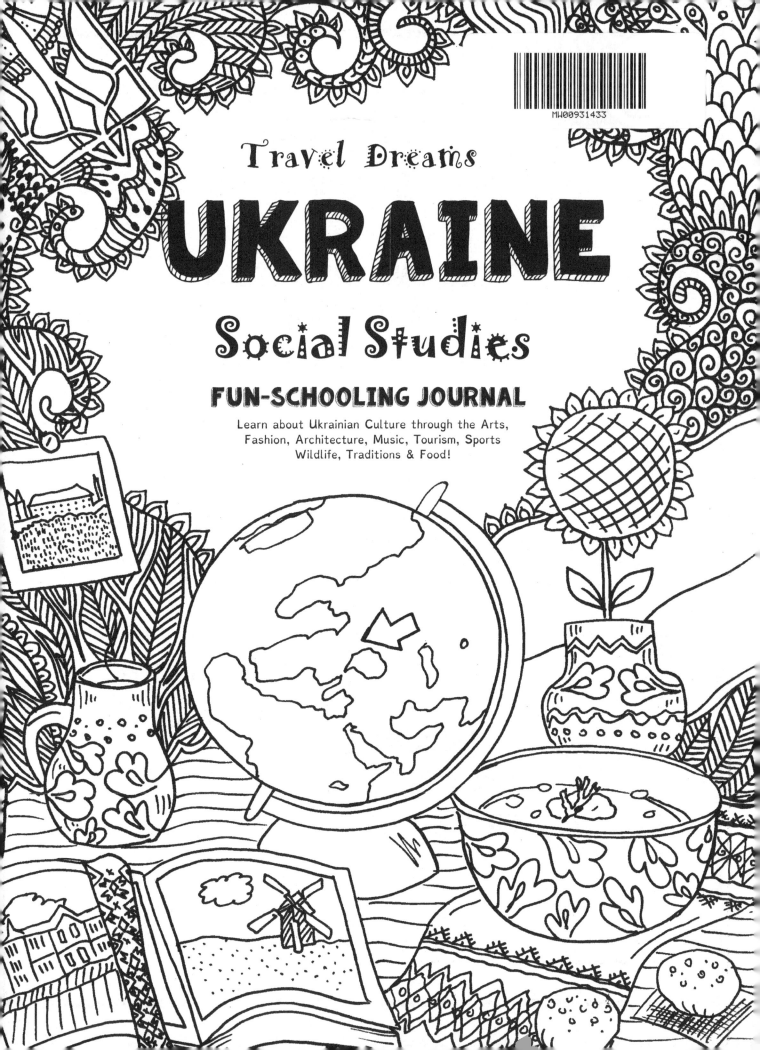

Travel Dreams

UKRAINE

Social Studies

FUN-SCHOOLING JOURNAL

Learn about Ukrainian Culture through the Arts,
Fashion, Architecture, Music, Tourism, Sports
Wildlife, Traditions & Food!

To hear traditional music from this country listen to

Travel Dreams Geography

AROUND THE WORLD IN 14 SONGS

Search for Amazon Product Number: B072C2QXJS

Around the world in 14 songs is a delightful musical tour of the world. Adults and children will enjoy these original instrumental songs that reflect the authentic style of music that originated on all six major continents. Travel to the rhythm and melody of traditional instruments, and enjoy the fun-filled tunes.

The musical journey begins in Ireland, sweeps across Europe, dances through Asia and Africa and then soars over the ocean to Australia and the Caribbean! After an exciting night at a Smoky Mountain bluegrass festival you will enjoy a siesta in Mexico and finally land in Brazil where you will join the festa in Rio-De-Janeiro.

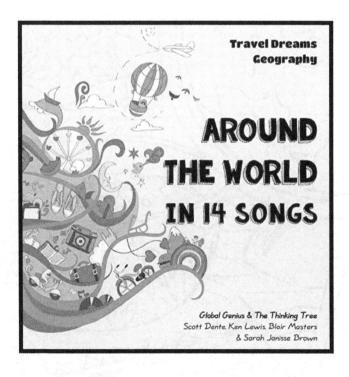

Travel Dreams Geography

AROUND THE WORLD IN 14 SONGS

*Global Genius & The Thinking Tree
Scott Dente, Ken Lewis, Blair Masters
& Sarah Janisse Brown*

Music has never been more fun... or educational!

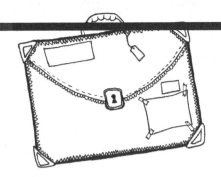

Travel Dreams
UKRAINE
FUN-SCHOOLING
JOURNAL

An Adventurous Approach
Social Studies

Learn about Ukrainian Culture through the Arts,
Fashion, Architecture, Music, Tourism, Sports
Wildlife, Traditions & Food!

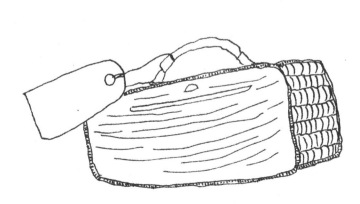

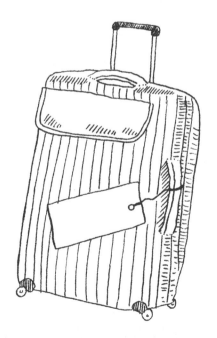

Travel Dreams
UKRAINE
Fun-Schooling
Journal

Name:

Date:

Contact Information:

About Me:

Let's Learn!

Topics & Activities You Can Explore With This Curriculum:

- Ethnic Cooking
- Travel
- History of Interesting Places
- How People Live
- Tourism
- Transportation
- Wildlife and Natural Wonders
- Cultural Traditions
- Natural Disasters

- Famous and Interesting People
- Missionary Stories
- Scientific Discoveries
- Fashion
- Architecture
- Plants
- Animals
- Maps
- Language

UKRAINE

Travel Dreams Fun-School Journal

You are going to learn about Ukraine

Teacher & Parent To-Do List:

- Plan a trip to Ukraine or just plan a trip to the library or local bookstore.
- Download Google Earth so your child can zoom in and learn more!
- Choose online videos about Ukraine so your child can learn about culture, food, tourism, traditions and history.
- Be prepared to help your child choose an ethnic recipe and shop for the ingredients.

Go to the Library or Bookstore to Pick Out:

- Books about Ukraine
- One Atlas or Book of Maps
- One Colorful Cookbook with Recipes from Ukraine

COLOR IN UKRAINE ON THE MAP

Zoom into Ukraine using Google Earth and explore
the wonders of this amazing country!

LABEL THE MAP

Add 15 Interesting Things to this Map!

Write or Draw

Use your Library Books

Popular Foods:	Traditional Clothing:
Draw the Flag:	A Quote or Proverb:
A Historic Event:	A Famous Landmark:

LEARNING TIME

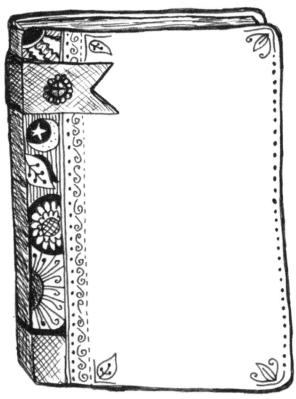

READ A BOOK AND WATCH A VIDEO ABOUT FOOD IN UKRAINE:

BOOK TITLE:_____
_____
VIDEO TITLE: _____
_____

What did you learn?
_____
_____
_____
_____
_____
_____

UKRAINIAN CUISINE

What do Ukrainians love to eat?

Can you list **5** of the most
popular Ukrainian dishes?

1. _____

2. _____

3. _____

4. _____

5. _____

6. _____

Draw your favorite Ukrainian food

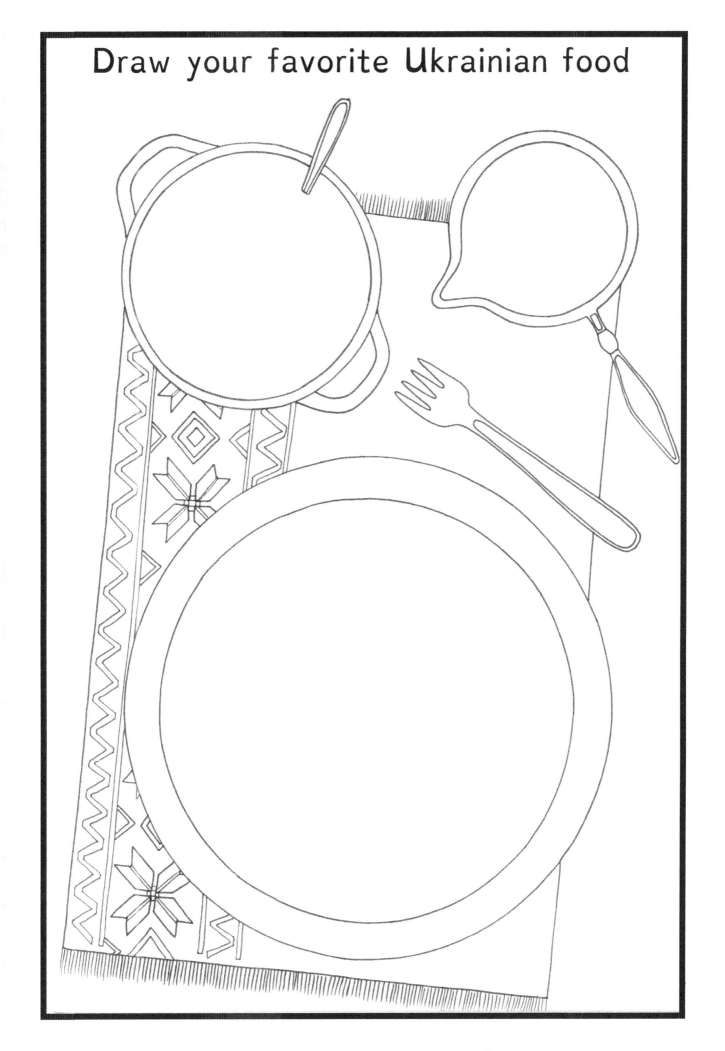

Find a Recipe From

UKRAINE

TITLE:

_____

Ingredients:

_____ _____

_____ _____

_____ _____

_____ _____

_____ _____

Instructions:

_____

_____

_____

_____

_____

_____

_____

_____

_____

Step by Step Food Prep:

1	2
3	4
5	6

DRAW THE FOOD THAT YOU PREPARED!

RATE THE RESULTS!
1, 2, 3, 4, 5

Color the words that best describe your food:

DELICIOUS

YUMMY

TASTY

GREAT

DELIGHTFUL

OKAY

BLAH!

GROSS

YUCKY

DISGUSTING

STINKY

ICKY

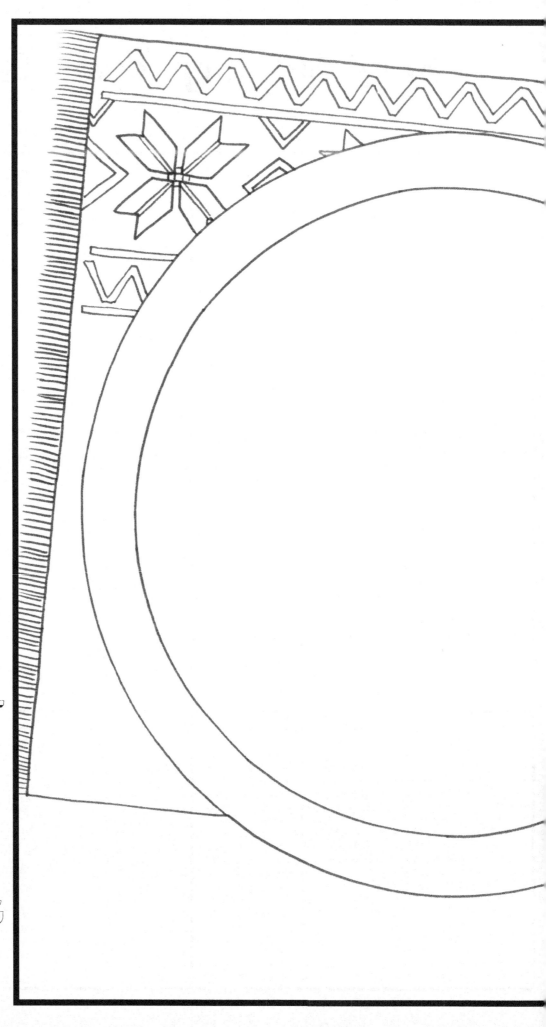

What to Do in Ukraine

Create a **COMIC STRIP** showing your dream adventure!

LEARNING TIME

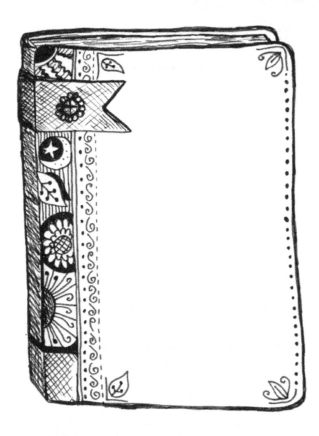

READ A BOOK AND WATCH A VIDEO ABOUT A FAMOUS PERSON

BOOK TITLE:_____
_____
VIDEO TITLE: _____
_____
_____

Write 3 Interesting Biography Facts

_____
_____
_____
_____
_____
_____

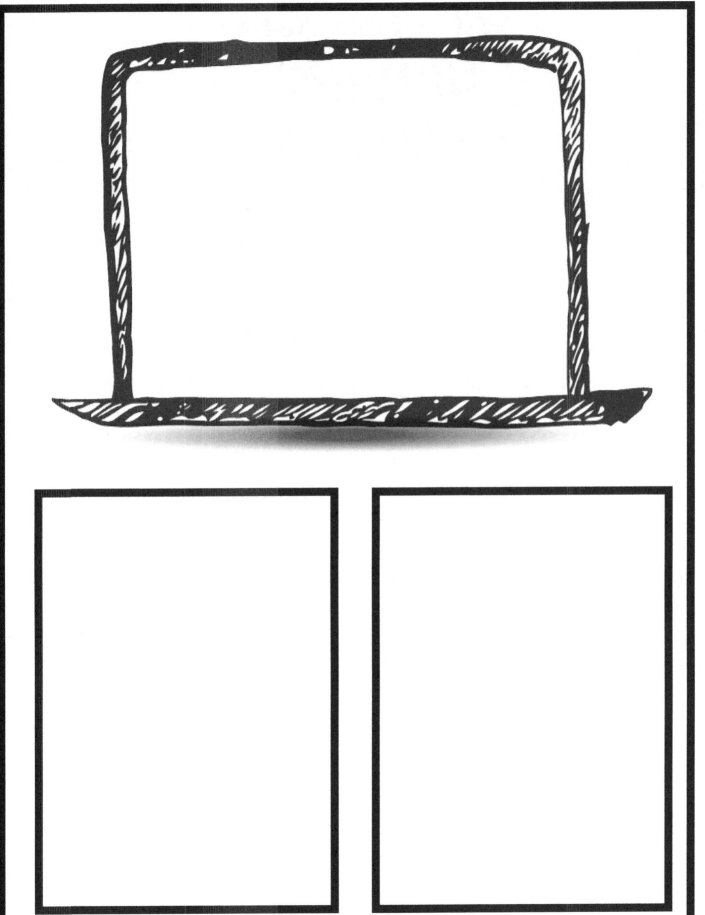

UKRAINE

Fashion in the City

_____

_____

_____

MODERN STYLES

Draw yourself dressed like a stylish Ukrainian :

Color The Traditional Costume:

Trace and color this
traditional Female Ukrainian costume

Trace and color this
traditional Male Ukrainian Costume

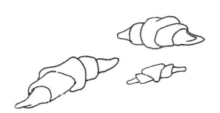

UKRAINIAN HISTORY

Write about a Historic Event

_____

_____

_____

_____

_____

_____

_____

_____

_____

_____

_____

_____

_____

_____

LEARNING TIME

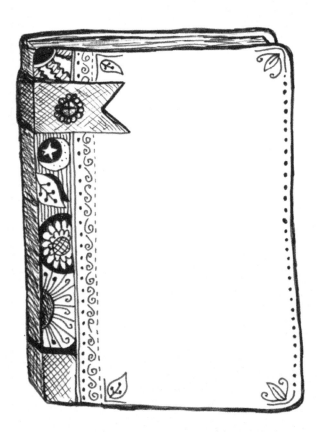

READ A BOOK AND WATCH A VIDEO ABOUT NATURE & WILDLIFE

BOOK TITLE:_____
_____
VIDEO TITLE: _____
_____
_____

Notes:

WHat ANiMaLS LiVe iN UKRaiNe?
CaN you LiSt teN?

1. _____
2. _____
3. _____
4. _____
5. _____
6. _____
7. _____
8. _____
9. _____
10. _____

Draw each of the animals

PLANTS IN UKRAINE

Can you list ten flowers or trees found in Ukraine?

1. _____
2. _____
3. _____
4. _____
5. _____
6. _____
7. _____
8. _____
9. _____
10. _____

Draw each of the plants

HISTORY OF MUSIC IN UKRAINE

Write about a famous Ukrainian musician:

_____

_____
_____
_____
_____
_____
_____
_____

What instrument did he/she play?

_____

Can you draw it?

A NATIONAL INSTRUMENT

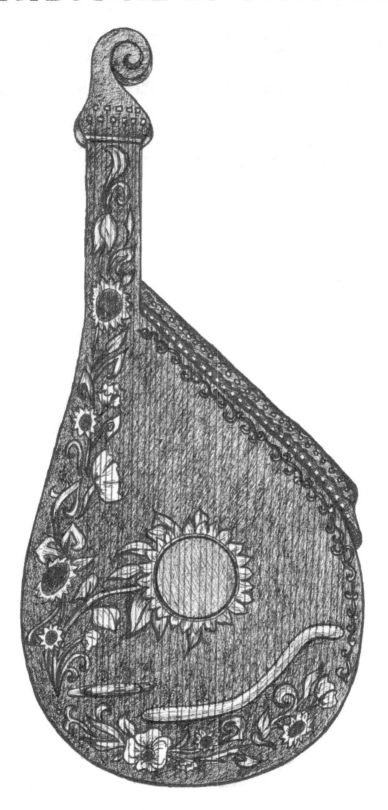

To hear traditional music from this country listen to
Travel Dreams Geography—Around the World in 14 Songs

Track Number & Song Name:
04-Ukraine - Sasha's Song

UKRAINIAN ART & ENTERTAINMENT

Read a book or watch a documentary about art and entertainment in Ukraine

Write down 5 interesting things you learned :

1. _____
   _____

2. _____
   _____

3. _____
   _____

4. _____
   _____

5. _____
   _____

Draw or doodle in Ukrainian style

Write doWN a quote or a Lyric FroM a FaMouS UkraiNiaN poeM or a SoNg

_____

_____

_____

_____

_____

_____

_____

_____

_____

_____

_____

_____

_____

_____

HISTORY OF TRANSPORTATION IN UKRAINE

Find 3 interesting facts about Ukrainian transportation

1. _____

_____

_____

2. _____

_____

_____

3. _____

_____

_____

Use your imagination and add something to this picture.

Write a short story about this picture

_____

_____

_____

_____

_____

_____

_____

_____

_____

UKRAINIAN INVENTIONS

Read a book or watch a documentary about your favorite Ukrainian inventor:

_____

Write down 5 interesting things about his/her life:

1. _____

2. _____

3. _____

4. _____

5. _____

Write down 3 Ukrainian inventions that changed the world:

1. _____

2. _____

3. _____

Draw your Favorite Ukrainian invention

UKRAINIAN ATHLETES

Read a book or watch a documentary about your favorite Ukrainian Athlete:

_____

Write down 5 interesting things about his/her life:

1. _____

2. _____

3. _____

4. _____

5. _____

Draw your Favorite Ukrainian Sport

UKRAINIAN HOMES
Write about a Family tradition in Ukraine

_____

_____

_____

_____

UKRAINIAN TRADITIONS
Draw some traditional Ukrainian décor elements

Trace & Color
A TRADITIONAL UKRAINIAN HOME

Design Your Own
UKRAINIAN HOME

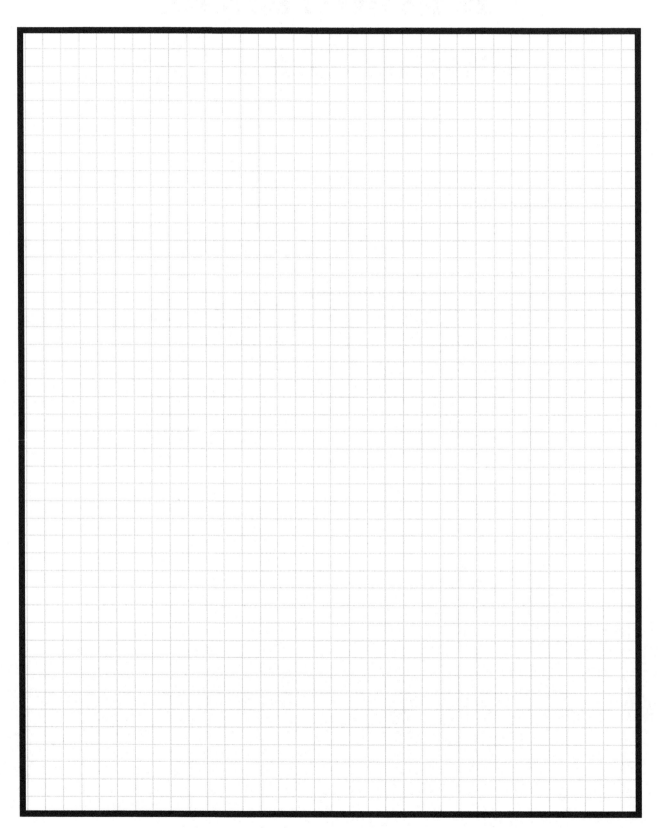

FiNd aNd cOLOr iN tHe HiddeN objects

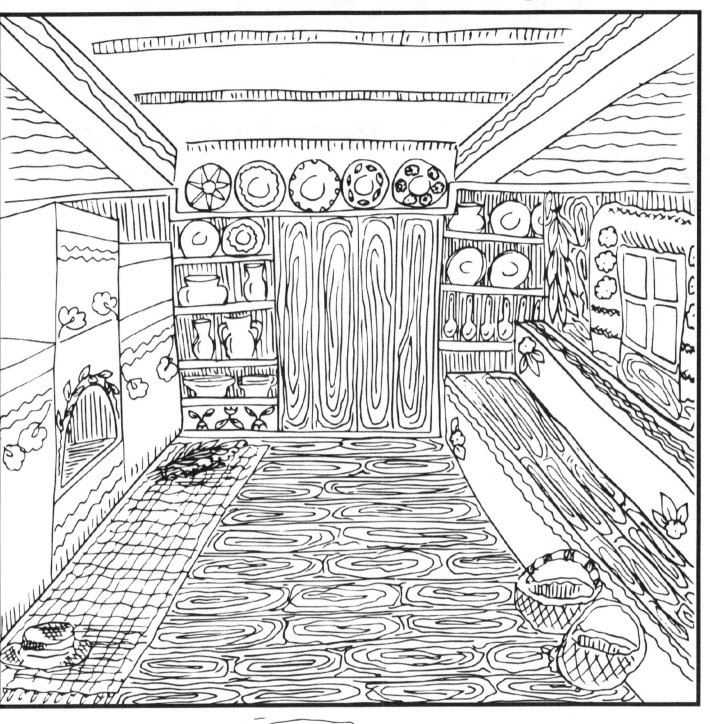

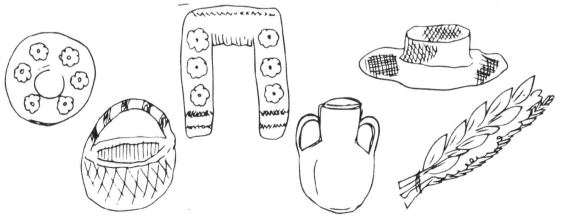

LEARNING TIME

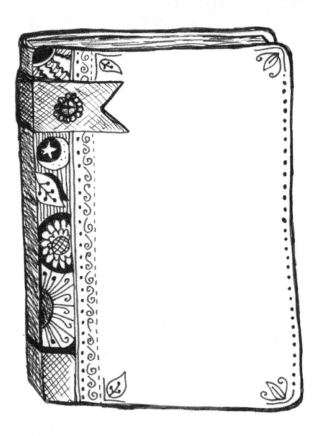

READ A BOOK AND WATCH A VIDEO ABOUT TOURISM & TRAVEL

BOOK TITLE:_____
_____
VIDEO TITLE: _____
_____
_____

Notes:
_____
_____
_____
_____
_____
_____

PLAN A TRIP TO THE CAPITAL OF UKRAINE

_ _ _ _

Who are you going with?

_____

What are you taking with you?

_____

How long is your trip?

_____

What do you want to see or visit?

_____

PLAN YOUR TRIP
What to Do in
Kiev

Five Things to Know
when Traveling to
UKRAINE

1 _____

2 _____

3 _____

4 _____

5 _____

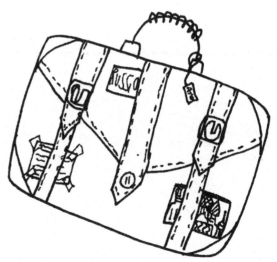

What to Say

Create a **COMIC STRIP** using six Ukrainian phrases:

CREATIVE WRITING

Write a story about an imaginary trip to Ukraine

Illustrate your Story

Do it Yourself
HOMESCHOOL
JOURNALS
BY THE THINKING TREE, LLC

FunSchoolingBooks.com

DyslexiaGames.com

Contact Us: jbrown@DyslexiaGames.com

Made in the USA
Las Vegas, NV
07 August 2022